LIFE IN THE
OCEANS

Written by **Lucy Baker**

Consultant Roger Hammond
Director of Living Earth

SCHOLASTIC INC.
New York Toronto London Auckland Sydney

ISBN 0-590-46132-X

30 29 28 27   5 6 / 0

Printed in the U.S.A.   08

First Scholastic printing, October 1992

Photograph Credits:
p.4 Greenpeace/Morgan p.5 Ardea/François Gohier p.7 Ardea/Ron & Valerie Taylor p.8–9 ZEFA/Dr D. James p.10 Planet Earth/Robert Arnold p.11 (top) Oxford Scientific Films/ Peter Parks (bottom) Oxford Scientific Films/Peter Parks p.12 (top) Ardea/J.-M. Labat (bottom) Oxford Scientific Films/G.I. Bernard p.13 (top left) Planet Earth/Peter David (top right) Planet Earth/Gillian Lythgoe (bottom) Planet Earth/Peter Scoones p.14 Ardea/Ron & Valerie Taylor p.15 Planet Earth/Peter David p. 16 Ardea/Clem Haagner p.17 (top) Planet Earth/Jim Brandenburg (bottom) Ardea/François Gohier p.18–19 B. & C. Alexander p.20 Ardea/Richard Vaughan p.21 ZEFA p.22–23 Ardea/François Gohier
Front cover: Ardea/François Gohier. Back cover: Tony Stone Worldwide/Mike Smith

Illustrations by Francis Mosley. Artworking by Claire Legemah.

CONTENTS

LOOKING AT THE OCEANS

Over two-thirds of the world's surface is covered by vast oceans, the oldest and largest living **environments**. Life began here more than 3.5 billion years ago. Without the fertile oceans, the earth would be dry, barren, and devoid of life.

Beneath the world's oceans lie rugged mountains, active volcanoes, vast plateaus, and almost bottomless **trenches**. The deepest ocean trenches could easily swallow up the tallest mountains on land.

Seen from above, the world's oceans appear empty and unchanging, but beneath the surface hides a unique world where water takes the place of air. A fantastic and rich assortment of plants and animals lives in these waters, from the microscopic **plankton** to the giant blue whale.

DID YOU KNOW?

● Salt is not the only substance found in seawater. There are also tiny traces of gold, silver, uranium, and other valuable **minerals**.

● Sound travels through water five times faster than through air. Some sea animals, such as dolphins, navigate through the oceans by bouncing sounds off their surroundings and listening to their **echo**.

● Although oceans dominate the world map, we have only just begun to explore their hidden depths. The deepest part of the ocean was first visited in 1960.

▶ There are no boundaries in the ocean. Animals can travel freely through the water. Most sea animals breathe underwater but some, like the dolphins and whales, need to come up for air every few minutes.

◀ In the tropics the oceans are warm and clear, but around the North and South Poles it is very cold; here, parts of the ocean are frozen all year long. Huge chunks of ice, called icebergs, float in these seas.

DIVIDING THE SEAS

In truth there is only one ocean. It stretches from the North Pole to the South Pole and encircles the globe. However, because the **continents** loosely divide the water, four separate oceans are recognized – the Pacific, the Atlantic, the Indian, and the Arctic. Within these oceans are smaller bodies of water called seas, **bays** and **gulfs** that are cut off from the open oceans by land formations.

The Pacific is the largest and deepest of the four great oceans. it covers more of the world's surface than all of the continents put together. The word Pacific means peaceful, but the water can be very rough. Waves over 35m (112 feet) tall have been recorded in the Pacific Ocean.

The Atlantic is the second biggest ocean and the busiest. Ships regularly cross the Atlantic waters carrying cargo between the Americas, Africa, and countries in Europe.

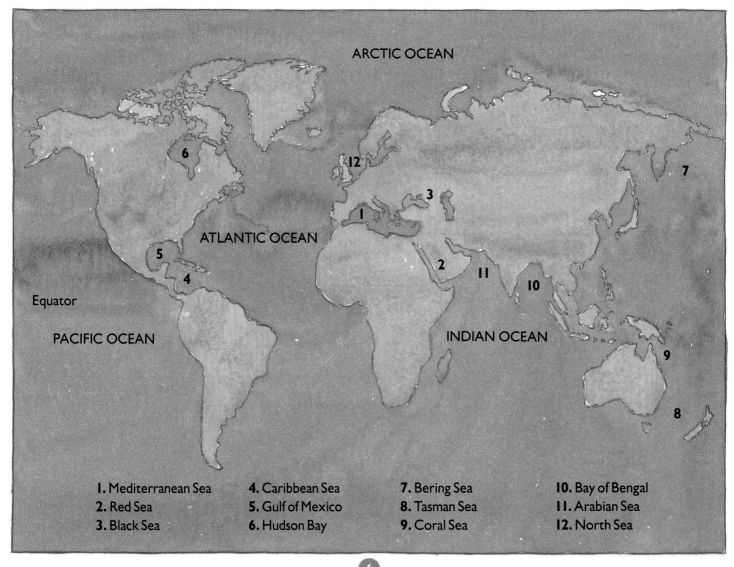

ARCTIC OCEAN

ATLANTIC OCEAN

Equator

PACIFIC OCEAN

INDIAN OCEAN

1. Mediterranean Sea	4. Caribbean Sea	7. Bering Sea	10. Bay of Bengal
2. Red Sea	5. Gulf of Mexico	8. Tasman Sea	11. Arabian Sea
3. Black Sea	6. Hudson Bay	9. Coral Sea	12. North Sea

DID YOU KNOW?

● One drop of seawater may travel through all the world's oceans in 5,000 years.

● The Atlantic Ocean is growing and the Pacific Ocean is shrinking. The world's continents move a few inches each year. This means that the relative sizes of the oceans are always changing.

● Greek divers are known to have reached depths of 22–30.5m (75–100 feet) in search of sponges, coral, and other treasures. When a diver ran short of breath, he would poke his head into a special weighted diving bell, filled with air from the surface.

● In several countries around the world the legend is told of a lost continent called Atlantis. This land is supposed to have lain in the Atlantic Ocean and was swallowed up by the sea after earthquakes and floods.

▲ In warm, tropical seas where the water is shallow and clear, there are vast, rocky structures known as **coral reefs**. These are the handiwork of small sea animals called polyps. Coral reefs are the **marine** equivalent of the rainforests. They hold a greater variety of life than any other part of the oceans.

MOVING WAVES

The world's oceans are always on the move. They travel in well-defined circular patterns called ocean **currents**. The currents flow like rivers, carrying warm water from the tropics and cold water from the **poles**. Where two currents meet, the colder water sinks, pushing warmer water up to the surface.

Besides the ocean currents, there is also the regular movement of the **tides**. Twice a day, all around the world, the oceans rise and fall along the coastlines. Scientists do not fully understand how the tides work, but they know they are linked to the pull on the earth by the moon and the sun.

The continual movement of the oceans is important to marine life. The tides and currents carry food from one part of the ocean to another. They stir up the water and produce small bubbles of oxygen which the ocean animals need to breathe.

In the Northern Hemisphere the ocean currents travel in a clockwise direction. In the Southern Hemisphere, they travel counterclockwise. The wind is the driving force behind the ocean's currents.

OCEAN POWER

Giant whirlpools or maelstroms can occur where two rushing currents are forced through narrow channels. These turbulent waters can wreck small sailing vessels.

Earthquakes and volcanic eruptions under the surface of the ocean can cause huge waves to speed through the water and explode on the shore. These giant waves are often called tidal waves but their proper name is tsunamis.

FOOD FOR LIFE

Plants provide the basic food for life in the ocean, just as they do on land. Plants that grow underwater are called algae, and there are two main groups found in the oceans.

The most familiar ocean algae are the seaweeds found around our coastlines. Limpets, periwinkles, and other shoreline creatures graze on seaweeds, but these are not available to the animals of the open ocean.

The most important marine plants are called phytoplankton. These tiny, floating plants grow wherever sunlight penetrates the water. Huge clouds of phytoplankton drift in the upper layers of the ocean, but they are too small to be seen with the naked eye.

Floating alongside and feeding upon the phytoplankton are tiny animals called zooplankton. This rich mix of plant and animal life, called plankton, is the foundation of all marine life.

PLANKTON FACTS

● Sailors crossing the ocean at night often see a soft glow on the water's surface. This is because some plankton produce flashes of blue–green light when they are disturbed.

● Very early lifeforms probably looked similar to today's phytoplankton.

● The largest animals in the world feed on plankton. Blue whales can weigh over 150 tons and be over 30.48m (100 feet) long. They sieve krill, tiny plankton animals, from the ocean waters through a curtain of whalebone inside their mouth.

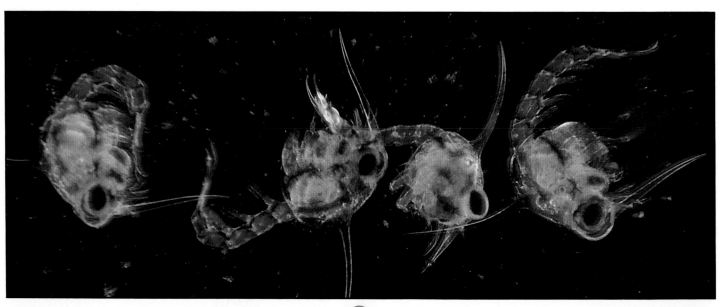

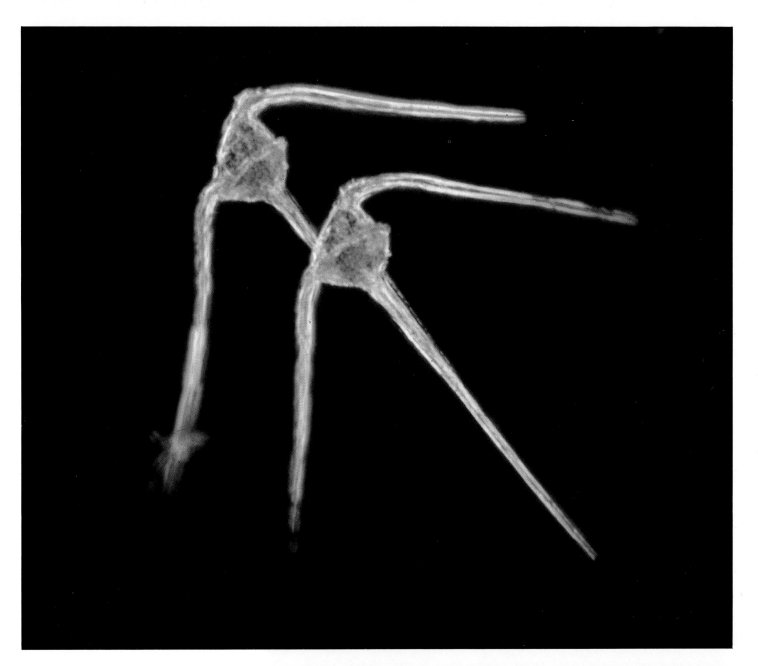

▲▶ Many of the tiny floating plants that make up the phytoplankton join together to make chains and bracelets. Others float alone and look like small pill boxes, sea shells, pencils, ice picks, or ribbons.

◀ Some members of the zooplankton are simple, single-celled lifeforms but many are the tiny larvae of fish, crabs, starfish, and other sea animals.

ALL SHAPES AND SIZES

There is a staggering variety of animals living in the world's oceans. Their size, shape, and color change enormously. To some extent, each marine animal's appearance depends on its lifestyle and where in the ocean it lives. Sea anemones and sponges, for instance, usually stay rooted to the ocean floor for their entire adult lives and look more like plants than animals.

Fishes are the most familiar marine creatures, but even their looks can be deceptive. Some species, like eels and pipefish, look more like worms or snakes than fish. Others, like the delicate sea horse, seem like a different sort of animal altogether.

▲ Many sea animals are transparent or a silvery-blue color, but some have bright, bold markings. The most colorful animals live in clear tropical waters. Their striking appearance helps them to establish territory and frighten off would-be attackers.

◄ The octopus is one of many curious sea animals. It has eight arms and a short, rounded body. Many octopuses live on the ocean floor where they hide among rocks and grab passing animals with their long, suckered arms. To swim, octopuses squirt water from a special siphon in their bodies.

▲ It is cold, black, and very still in the deepest parts of the ocean. Many animals living there have a light on their body that they use to attract prey. The deep-sea angler fish, above, are very strange. If the male of the species meets his mate, he attaches himself to her body. After a time, his body breaks down and he becomes no more than a sperm bag used to fertilize the female's eggs.

▲ Sponges encrust rocks, corals, and vegetation on the sea floor, from the shallowest coastlines to the deepest trenches. There are over 3,500 marine sponges. Some form fleshy sheets, others upright chimney stacks. Sponges sieve dead and decaying matter from the water around them.

▶ The blue-spotted sting ray is a close relative of the shark. It floats over the surface of the seabed, feeding on slugs, worms, and other sea animals.

THE HUNTER AND THE HUNTED

Many marine animals spend their entire lives sifting the water for plankton, but they in turn are hunted by other animals. It is estimated that for every ten plankton-feeders at least one hunter lurks nearby.

One of the most notorious marine hunters is the shark. Sharks have a reputation as man-eaters, but of the 200 varieties only 25 are in fact dangerous to people. Sharks are perfect killing machines. Their bodies are streamlined for a fast-moving, hunting life, and their mouths are lined with razor-sharp teeth.

Not all marine hunters are as fearsome as the sharks. The pretty sea anemones look harmless, but they trap animals in their feathery tentacles and inject poison into their victim's body.

DEFENSE FACTS

Octopuses and cuttlefish squirt ink into the face of their attacker. This gives them time to get away.

Flying fish leap out of the water to escape their enemies.

Many sea animals, like clams and oysters, live in shells. The shells provide a home and act as armor, protecting the animal's soft body.

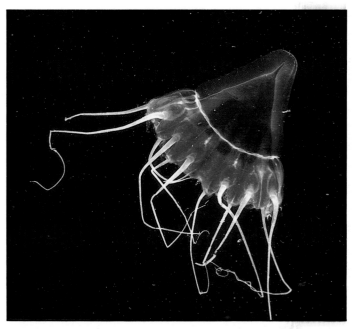

▲ Jellyfish, like sea anemones, catch animals in their trailing tentacles and then poison them. Some of the most powerful poisons in the natural world are produced by jellyfish.

◄ Sharks race through the water, chasing their prey of fish, seals, turtles, small whales, other sharks, and even sea birds. Even when they are not chasing their next meal, sharks must keep moving all the time or they begin to sink.

TAKING TO THE WATER

During the long passage of time, a small procession of land animals has returned to the oceans for its livelihood. Reptiles, mammals, and even birds have braved the deep, salty waters to take advantage of the rich bounty of sea life.

Whales, seals, turtles, and penguins are some of the animals that have left dry land to colonize the oceans. These creatures cannot breathe underwater like true sea animals so they regularly visit the water's surface for air. Whales are the most successful ocean colonizers. People often mistake them for fish. Whales spend their entire lives in the water, but most animals that have taken to the water must come ashore to **reproduce**.

▼ Many birds are called sea birds because they live on coastlines or on remote islands and rely on the oceans for their food. However, one bird in particular has mastered life in the oceans. The penguin spends most of its time swimming in cold waters, chasing fish and other sea animals.

▲ Animals are still turning to the world's oceans. Polar bears are considered to be marine mammals because they spend most of their time on or in the frozen Arctic Ocean hunting seals. They are expert swimmers and their wide, furry paws are webbed to help them move through the water.

▶ Sea reptiles like turtles are restricted to warm parts of the world's oceans. They leave the water to lay their eggs on sandy beaches.

OCEAN RESOURCES

People cannot live in the world's oceans, but they have always harvested the rich waters. As the human population has increased, people have turned to the oceans more and more for food and raw materials. Today over 70 billion kg (70 million tons) of fish are caught each year and one-fifth of the world's oil and gas is mined from the seabed.

Modern fishing methods are often so intensive that they devastate fish communities and upset the balance of ocean life. Many of yesterday's most fertile seas are no longer able to support large fishing fleets because the fish stocks are so low.

The nets used by many of today's fishermen can also cause problems. They are made of nylon and do not rot underwater. If they are lost overboard, these nets become death traps to seals, dolphins, and other marine creatures that cannot detect them.

Fish are not the only animals people take from the ocean. Crabs and lobsters are two of our many seafood products. Sponges are chipped off the ocean floor and end up in bathrooms all over the world. Some seals and whales have been hunted to extinction for their meat, fur, and oil.

▼ Fishing is big business. Every day thousands of boats drag nets through the oceans to catch fish and other sea animals. This North Sea trawler is small compared to the largest fishing vessels. The world's supertrawlers can be over 90m (295 feet) long.

● Fish oils are used to make glues, soaps, and margarines.

● A rare gem called a **pearl** is formed inside the shells of certain oysters.

● Big nodules of iron, copper, and manganese are lifted from the seabed using special suction pumps or are raked into nets by dredging machines.

● In dry lands, seawater is sometimes treated to create a fresh water supply.

● Seaweed can be eaten like a vegetable and is also used in ice cream, toothpaste, paints, medicines, and other everyday products.

MAKING THE SEA SICK

Although we rely on the world's oceans for food, we treat them like garbage dumps and sewers. Waste is pumped and dumped into the water, and **pesticides** and other man-made **pollutants** are washed into the ocean by rivers and streams.

The pollution of the world's oceans is harmful. Many sea animals are injured, strangled, or suffocated each year because of floating debris called flotsam. The high level of **toxic** wastes in a few seas is poisoning some animals and driving others away.

Land-locked seas like the Mediterranean are among the most polluted, but coastal waters everywhere are affected by the waste.

▶ Busy ports can become virtual deserts of the ocean world. The oil, sewage, and litter spilled into the water make a harbor unfit for sea life.

▲ Oil spills threaten marine life. This poor sea bird will probably die unless the oil is cleaned from its feathers.

POLLUTION PROBLEMS

● Sealed barrels of dangerous radioactive and chemical waste have been dumped in some oceans, but no one knows if the containers are safe in the watery conditions.

● In some places around the world the local seafood is unfit to eat.

SAVE THE OCEANS

Countries around the world are beginning to realize the importance of the oceans. International laws have been made to restrict the amount of waste put into the water, and some marine mammals are now protected. Countries on the shores of the dirtiest seas have started major clean-up programs.

There is still a lot to be done. We need to understand patterns of marine life if we are to avoid overfishing and preserve future fish stocks. In recent years, enormous damage has been caused in some oceans by oil tankers spilling their deadly cargo. Oil blocks out light from the ocean, upsetting plankton production and so affecting all marine life. Through public pressure, oil companies could be persuaded to buy safer boats that would not leak in an accident.

Seemingly harmless activities in the oceans have now been found to have damaging effects on marine life. The electric cables that criss-cross the ocean floor disturb some seabed creatures and confuse many fish. Sharks bite into the cables, mistaking them for prey. The noise from boats, busy coastal resorts, and ocean-based industries frighten away seals, dolphins, and other animals from their traditional breeding grounds.

Whales have become a strong international symbol of ocean conservation. These extraordinary creatures have lived in the oceans far longer than people have lived on land. They are giants of the natural world.

Whales have been hunted for their oils and meat for so long that they are now difficult to find.

Most people agree that we must not kill any more whales, and laws have been made to protect the largest species. A few countries, however, continue to hunt whales and eat their meat as an expensive delicacy.

DAKUWACA FIGHTS FOR HIS LIFE

For thousands of years people have told stories about the world about them. Often these stories try to explain something that people do not really understand, like how the world began or where light comes from. This tale is told by the people of Fiji who depend on the ocean which surrounds them for food and transportation.

Long ago the sharks were the rulers of the islands that make up Fiji in the Pacific Ocean. Each island had its own particular shark who lived beside the reef entrance of the island. These sharks patrolled the waters of their territory, challenging anyone who dared to come near. They allowed friends in but fought with hostile sharks until they paid a tribute.

Dakuwaca thought himself the greatest of all the sharks. He was big and fierce and enjoyed nothing better than a fight with another shark. He had never lost a fight and he was quite sure he never would. He cared nothing for the terrible storms which his fights caused, whipping up the waters so that the islanders were tossed about in their boats. Often island houses were swept away by massive waves from the ocean.

Dakuwaca was patrolling his reef one day when he came across a shark called Masilaca. Masilaca was the mischief maker among the sharks. He did not fight much himself but, with his wily ways, he had caused more fights than most sharks had fought!

"Good day, Dakuwaca," he said. "I suppose you're off for another fight. It's amazing, the way you always beat the other sharks. I wish I were as good a fighter as you."

"No other shark is as good a fighter as I am," said Dakuwaca. "Hardly anyone bothers to challenge me any more. They all know that I am so much stronger than them. In fact it's getting very dull around here."

"Perhaps if you want a really good fight, you should go over to Kandavu Island. I hear there's a creature well worth fighting there, a mighty monster which guards the reef so that it is impossible to go near it. But no one ever goes there because they are much too afraid of the creature," said Masilaca, with a sly glint in his eye. "Of course *I'm* not suggesting that you're frightened, you're much too brave and strong. And I'm sure none of the other sharks think that you're afraid either."

Dakuwaca thrashed his tail through the water. Of course he wasn't afraid, what a suggestion! But if the other sharks thought he was afraid, he had better do something at once. Almost before Masilaca had finished speaking, Dakuwaca set off towards Kandavu, determined to challenge the fearsome monster.

As Dakuwaca approached Kandavu, he heard a deep, powerful voice calling from the shore. Dakuwaca had never heard anything like it before, and he found himself trembling a little.

"How foolish," he told himself. "Nothing on the shore can harm me." And he swam on.

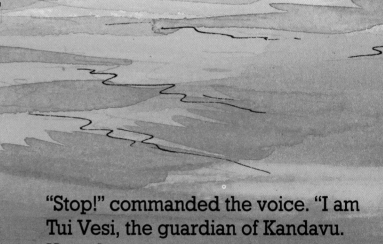

"Stop!" commanded the voice. "I am Tui Vesi, the guardian of Kandavu. How dare you approach my precious island so boldly."

Dakuwaca was rather frightened, but determined not to show it.

"And I am Dakuwaca, the greatest of all sharks. Come out and fight to defend your island."

"I am a land guardian and so cannot come into the water to fight you," said Tui Vesi. "I shall send one of my servants to fight you instead. But be warned! It is a great and terrible monster, and it would be much better if you left now."

"No one is braver or stronger than I," said Dakuwaca. "I am not afraid of anything. I will fight your servant."

He swam around the mouth of the reef, watching and waiting for his opponent. His body was strong and quick and his teeth were sharp.

Suddenly a giant arm appeared from the reef and grabbed him. A giant octopus! This wasn't what Dakuwaca was expecting at all! He thrashed and twisted to rid himself of the arm. His sharp teeth were quite useless because he could not bend his body to bite at the arm. The arm loosened as he twisted and, for a moment, Dakuwaca thought he was free. But no, two more arms whipped around, so that he could no longer move at all. And the arms began to squeeze, tighter and tighter until Dakuwaca could bear it no longer.

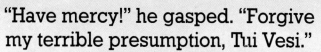

"Have mercy!" he gasped. "Forgive my terrible presumption, Tui Vesi."

The arms of the octopus loosened slightly, and Tui Vesi's mighty voice boomed out into the waters once more.

"I will release you, Dakuwaca, providing that you promise to guard the people of my island from sharks which might attack them when they go out in their canoes."

"Yes, yes! Of course I will," Dakuwaca agreed.

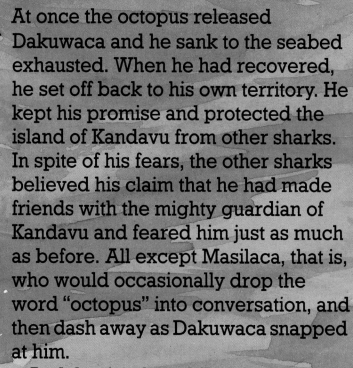

At once the octopus released Dakuwaca and he sank to the seabed exhausted. When he had recovered, he set off back to his own territory. He kept his promise and protected the island of Kandavu from other sharks. In spite of his fears, the other sharks believed his claim that he had made friends with the mighty guardian of Kandavu and feared him just as much as before. All except Masilaca, that is, who would occasionally drop the word "octopus" into conversation, and then dash away as Dakuwaca snapped at him.

And that is why, while other fishermen of the Fiji islands fear for their lives because of the sharks, the men of Kandavu ride happily in their canoes.

TRUE OR FALSE?

Which of these facts are true and which ones are false? If you have read this book carefully, you will know the answers.

1. Almost one-third of the world's surface is covered by oceans.

2. Dolphins and whales can stay underwater for several hours.

3. Sound travels through water five times faster than through air.

4. The world's four oceans are the Pacific, the Atlantic, the Mediterranean, and the Aegean.

5. It takes 5,000 years for one drop of seawater to travel through all the world's oceans.

6. Tsunamis are caused by underwater volcanic eruptions and earthquakes.

7. Plankton is a rich mixture made up of the debris from seaweed.

8. Blue whales are the largest animals in the world.

9. Octopuses have 12 arms and feed mainly on seals.

10. Sharks must keep moving all the time or they will sink.

11. Fish travel in schools until they have learned how to protect themselves.

12. The paws of a polar bear are webbed.

13. Seaweed is used in making ice cream.

GLOSSARY

Bay is a part of an ocean or other large body of water that forms a curve in the shoreline. It is bordered on the coastline by headlands or capes.

Continent is a large piece of land, or mainland. It is larger than a normal island and is usually divided into several countries (except for the continent of Australia). Two or more continents may be joined together by a narrow neck of land.

Current or stream is the movement of a body of water in a particular direction. Ocean currents may be very strong and extend over great distances.

Echo is the repetition of a noise caused by the bouncing back of sound waves from a solid object. Marine mammals such as dolphins use echoes to locate food and to avoid obstacles.

Coral reef is a colorful ridge formation, usually underwater. It is made up of the hard outer casing produced by a colony of millions of tiny animals known as polyps.

Environment is the set of conditions in the area where an animal lives. The animal's survival depends on how well it can respond to these conditions.

Extinction is when the last member of a species dies out. This may be due to overhunting by humans, the arrival of a rival animal or plant, or changes in the species' environment.

Gulf is a part of a sea or ocean that loops into the neighboring coastline. It is narrower at its mouth than a bay.

Land-locked means surrounded by land.

● **Marine** means connected with the sea. Marine animals are those that live in the sea.

● **Minerals** are chemical compounds found in rocks. Some of them are useful to humans and are mined.

● **Pearl** is a small gem, usually round and white, cream or bluish-gray. It slowly forms as a protective layer around a grain of sand or other object that irritates the soft flesh inside an oyster's shell.

● **Pesticides** are chemicals used to kill pests that feed on crops. Pesticides may sometimes be dangerous to creatures other than the pests they control.

● **Plankton** is the rich soup made up of many types of microscopic life. A large variety of sea animals feed on it.

● **Poles** are found at the exact north and south ends of the earth. Day and night each last six months here.

● **Pollutant** is a dirty and poisonous product such as car fumes that damages the environment.

● **Reproduction** is when adult creatures produce new, young individuals for the continuation of their species.

● **Tide** is the regular rise and fall of the sea. It is caused by the pull of the moon and the sun.

● **Toxic** means poisonous and harmful to life.

● **Trench** is a deep furrow. The Mariana Trench near Guam is the deepest known place in any ocean.

INDEX